ERMILO ABREU GÓMEZ was born in 1894. Novelist, poet, journalist, critic, scholar and educator, he taught in Mexico, the United States, and several Latin American universities and was active in the cultural activities of UNESCO and the Pan American Union. He died in 1971.

CANEK
HISTORY AND LEGEND OF A MAYA HERO

ERMILO ABREU GÓMEZ

Translated with an Introduction by
MARIO DÁVILA *and* CARTER WILSON

 A BARD BOOK/PUBLISHED BY AVON BOOKS

AVON BOOKS
A division of
The Hearst Corporation
959 Eighth Avenue
New York, New York 10019

Copyright © 1979 by The Regents of the University
of California
Published by arrangement with the author
Library of Congress Catalog Card Number: 75-32674
ISBN: 0-380-61937-7

First Bard Printing, February, 1983

BARD TRADEMARK REG. U. S. PAT. OFF. AND IN
OTHER COUNTRIES, MARCA REGISTRADA, HECHO EN
U. S. A.

Printed in the U. S. A.

OP   10 9 8 7 6 5 4 3 2 1

CONTENTS

Introduction | vii

The Writing of *Canek* | 1

CANEK | 3

    The Characters | 7

    Closeness | 13

    The Doctrine | 33

    Injustice | 47

    War | 56

Glossary | 67

INTRODUCTION

Hurrying through low bleached Mayan villages en route to the archeological remains at Chichén Itzá and Uxmal or the new temples to tourism on the white sands of Cancún, modern-day travelers are not likely to come across any signs of the fierce and bloody history of the Yucatán. The gentle demeanor and easy-seeming manner of the Mayan people obscures the tenacious, sometimes violent struggle they have waged to maintain the integrity of their culture.

The history of the peninsula has been a chronicle of oppression and resistance. From the victory of the Spanish in 1546 down to demonstrations of peasant dissatisfaction in the 1970's, the Yucatan has remained a divided land. One culture has dominated but never finally succeeded in "conquering" the other. There have been long periods of peace, of "fit," when the native and the colonial ways of life have seemed to be in complement. But like the dark waters of the labyrinth of underground rivers which crisscross the Yucatán, beneath the tranquil surface there always runs a deep current of opposition. Two views of the world, each complicated and vital in itself, remain in fundamental disharmony.

In 1940 a Yucatec-born writer and scholar named Ermilo Abreu Gómez published a short novel called *Canek*. It remains among the most vivid introductions to daily life in the Yucatán, and to the two conflicting visions of the world which have kept the peninsula off and on in turmoil for over four hundred years. In itself, *Canek* has a wonderful succinctness. Anyone attempting to introduce it should try to attain the same quality. What we offer here, then, is a sketched backdrop to the book: some indication of the major history of rebellion in the Yucatán, some possible reasons why Mayan people throughout Middle America have been disposed to risk everything for the sake of their autonomy, and a speculation on why Abreu Gómez's small story should have achieved the wide readership and honored durability which it has.

The Spanish imposed a new hierarchy and a new religion in the Yucatán. Spanish master and Catholic priest replaced Mayan noble and priest. The people became peasant workers on the vast haciendas such as the one where Canek and his young friend Guy live in the novel. In their efficiency, the Spanish saw no reason to change the things in the lives of their new subjects which had no effect on the subjects' immortal souls or their ability to do backbreaking work. Everyday existence in the village at the foot of the hacienda street probably did not seem so different from everyday village life before the Spanish ships arrived. The *batab* or village headman and his informal council of elders still made the decisions in the old language. The old rites and festivities continued and the old gods and spirits exercised their power and their charms behind the panoply of the new saints and saviors.

But the equilibrium of the colonial society was false. In the old order, ruler and ruled had shared values. Now between the Maya and their new masters there existed a wide chasm of cultural differences, a gap bridged only occasionally and imperfectly by sympathetic whites like Padre Matías in *Canek*. The Mayan peasant resisted as best he could the labor demands which encroached on the tasks of planting, weeding, and harvesting corn. The people opposed the excessive taxes and tributes which threatened their small margin of survival. Converts to the new faith, they were distressed by any sacrilegious changes in the new, now-sacred rituals. The irreverence of the whites toward the very land itself both frightened and offended them. Though they accepted the authority of their new masters, they felt a higher responsibility to protect the moral order of the world. Their sense of outrage and of righteousness is clear in written documents which survive from the Caste War:

> We poor Indians are aware of what the whites are doing to injure us, of how many injuries they commit against us, even to our children and harmless women. So much injury without basis seems to us a crime. Indeed, therefore, if the Indian revolt, it is because the whites gave them reason; because the

whites say they do not believe in Jesus Christ, because they burn the cornfield....*

Geography abetted the rebellious spirit. Though the Spanish control spread across much of the flat, northern territory of the peninsula, there was always a "frontier," an edge to colonial control. South in the jungles of the Petén of Guatemala, a fugitive Mayan group, the Itzá, established a rebel kingdom. For a century and a half after the pacification of the north, they gave refuge to malcontents and escapees from the hacienda system and successfully resisted domination. The Itzá kings took the hereditary name "Canek." Later the English in bordering British Honduras sold guns to Mayan rebels under the still-respected principle of foreign policy which reasons that any trouble made for one's neighbors is a good day's work for oneself.

The rebellion of 1761 brought to life in *Canek* was in reality a brief and terrible moment. The immediate cause was the murder of a white merchant during the drunken revelry of a fiesta in the frontier village of Cisteil. The local priest fled to a neighboring town with the news that the Indians were in revolt. The *batab* of Cisteil called in Maya from the surrounding countryside. The low stone walls which outline nearly every Mayan homesite were taken down and used to make barricades across the roads. The *batab* proclaimed himself king and assumed the name "Canek." It had been written in the *Chilam Balam,* the greatest of the books of Mayan prophesy, that a king of the Itzá would eventually return to drive the whites into the sea. But Canek's uprising was quickly squelched. Its leader was drawn and quartered in the plaza of the capital at Mérida, his body burned, and his ashes scattered to the wind. Eight of his captains were garroted and two hundred of his followers were each relieved of an ear to mark them as rebels.

Mayan people have a strong sense of continuity with their past. Their history, passed on mainly by word of mouth, becomes imbedded in stories and remains for them a living thing. Almost ninety years after the events at Cisteil, a new and more successful generation of Mayan rebels remembered: they took the name "Jacinto

*Quoted in Nelson Reed, *The Caste War of Yucatan* (Stanford University Press), p. 48.

Canek" as their rallying cry. The conflict which began in 1848 came to be called the "War of the Castes." In one form or another it lasted for more than fifty years. For several decades the Yucatán was a literally divided land. The whites occupied the territory around Mérida and the Maya, calling themselves the *Cruzob*, "people of the Cross," established a capital and a separate nation at Chan Santa Cruz in the southeast. Some historians maintain that the Caste War never actually concluded. The rebels retreated slowly, less before armies than before the encroachments of the railroad and "civilization," and eventually seemed to disappear in the chicle forests of Quintana Roo. Even today when there are local-level disturbances in the country towns of the Yucatán, the Mérida newspapers are quick to remind their readers of the Caste War and to raise the possibility that another version of it may be on the way.

What is particular to Mayan people which causes them, even into the 1970's, to continue to seek ways to throw off their oppressors? In *Canek*, without being didactic, Abreu Gómez indicates some possible answers to the difficult question.

By the time of the Spanish invasion, the Mayan region was fragmented into localized political groups. In central Mexico, the Conquistadores were able to assume control of the existing machinery of the Aztecs and other centralized states. In the Mayan areas there was no such mechanism available to them. The village was the principal unit of organization, and power was held locally by clusters of interrelated families. These loosely adhering civilian groups could be transformed almost overnight into military organizations with an agreed-upon hierarchy. The Maya, then, were prepared for battle even in times of peace. When Jacinto Canek sits down to a chat with his friends Domingo Canché and Ramón Balam, he is in some sense also convoking a council of war.

Abreu Gómez further makes it clear that for him it is their unique view of the world and their rightful place in it which gives Mayan people the ability to keep up the struggle against the dominant culture. They know themselves to be the true inheritors of their land: outsiders will come and they will go away. The Maya are thus free to act wholeheartedly and unselfconsciously to defend their way of life. In this crucial matter, they are not fettered by doubt either about their cause or their ultimate victory.

Although the whites transgress and offend the Mayan understanding of things, making inevitable the conflict between the cultures, in the tender relationship between Guy the Spanish boy and Canek the Indian rebel, Abreu Gómez affirms his own belief that the encompassing and balanced Mayan world view need not be alien to any man, white or Indian.

Ermilo Abreu Gómez was born in Mérida in 1894. In the relative political stability of the period, Mérida was becoming the center of an economic and cultural renaissance. The high life was paid for by profits from henequén, the so-called "green gold" of the Yucatán. As a young man, Abreu Gómez edited several literary journals and contributed to the burgeoning regional theater. Later, living in Mexico City, he became a major literary essayist and a scholarly authority on colonial literature. Influenced by the nationalist "indigenist" movement in Mexican politics and culture in the 1930's, Abreu Gómez returned in writing to a subject closer to home and, most likely, closer to his heart. In editions of the *Popol Vuh,* in short stories, and in his most popular work, *Canek,* he presented the world of the Mayan people of his homeland.

Among other things, *Canek* is a book lit by the special glow and elegaic quality which remembrances of childhood, of things otherwise lost, can strike in a writer. In his ingenuous recollection of how *Canek* came to be written, Abreu Gómez tells how as a boy he heard the legends and the lives of the Maya at firsthand. Like most children, he was an observant and careful ethnographer. Many of the customs described in *Canek*—for example, making a terrible racket during an eclipse to scare off whatever is engorging the moon—are still practiced today. The people he listened to as a child were sons and daughters of a well-remembered war, the oppression and resistance he was to write about forty years later a vital factor in their lives.

As a piece of fiction, a made thing, *Canek's* secret strength and beauty—and the secret of its popular success and durability—comes from its lack of apparent form. Instead of borrowing myths and legends from the rich Mayan oral tradition and shaping them into a novel in a format familiar to us, Abreu Gómez weaves together fragments he has garnered from a variety of sources. There are photographically sharp renderings of moments in the lazy day-to-day life of a colonial hacienda, borrowings from the prophetic insights of the ancient Mayan texts, little stories within the story (some of these so slight they disappear into nothingness). As a compendium of what seem to be found observations, *Canek* takes on the feel of being not only *about* a folk culture, but of being itself a "folk" document. The lack of shape, the irregularity of form, becomes a virtue instead of a fault. Fairly willingly readers surrender themselves to *Canek's* own special reality, its separateness from traditional categories of fiction, ethnography, history, or biography. In the language of today, *Canek* is a "simulation," a copying. But the trick, and the proof of Abreu Gómez's genius, is that he could imagine a simulation or an imitating of something which had not before existed.

The Maya continue to pass along through generations the tales of their struggle against their white lords. The existing written documents by rebel leaders are deeply eloquent indictments of their masters. But the tales and the complaints were not meant for outsiders. It remained for Abreu Gómez to provide a tapestry which lets other people throughout the world share in the richness and beauty of the folk culture of the Yucatán. At the same time, *Canek* is true enough to its origins so that a newly literate Mayan adult will sit down and read it cover to cover with that solemn pleasure and intensity which comes upon us when we encounter an image which seems to reflect or give back to us our very selves.

A glossary of Spanish and Mayan terms used in the text is appended to the present translation.

The translators stand in gratitude for various sorts of assistance to Geoffrey and Pamela Ashton, C. William Ballantyne, Hipolito Pech Mena, and Duane G. Metzger.

—Mario L. Dávila and Carter Wilson

THE WRITING OF
CANEK

Perhaps my friend the reader would like to know how this book came about. When I was a child I traveled with my father through the countryside of the Yucatán. While he went out about his business, I stayed behind at the inns among Mayan people.

In the evening after dinner, by the hearth in the kitchen, the men would start to recount the stories and legends of the area. One of them was about the like of Canek. His adventures and his sayings remained etched on my memory.

Later, as a student in school, I came upon the written accounts of Canek, which completed the engraving of his memory and his image onto my spirit.

Many years passed before the day that there appeared in my mind a framework which could embrace this hero's story. I began filling notebook after notebook with descriptions of scenes from his life. When I had a number of chapters done, I began to revise them and put them in order. One night, in the house of María Asúnsolo, I read the first draft of the book to a group of friends. Another time I read a newer version at the house of Silvestre Revueltas.

The first edition was illustrated by the engraver Abelardo Avila. To commemorate my fiftieth birthday, Manolo Altolaguirre produced another edition under the imprint of his press La Verónica. The poet José Carner included the tale in the volume *Héroes Mayas*. Another lovely edition was published by Antigua Librería Robredo with drawings by Alberto Beltrán. There is a shorter edition for children which was published in El Salvador.

So, in over twenty years, according to the records of the Biblioteca Nacional de México, what with various editions and reprintings, *Canek* has appeared over twenty times. It is also in the record series "Voz viva de México," produced by the Universidad Nacional with notes by Luis Rius. It was translated into German by Ludwig Renn, into English by David Heft, and a Russian version was published in Moscow. Now, I'm told, a Portuguese version is about to appear translated by Bolivar de Freitas. There are also two or three editions at large which, if they aren't real "pirates," are at least "privateers."*

As a sort of game I have let run through *Canek* something of my own life and also of the lives of others. The boy Guy is my alter ego —me changed into a gentle little wraith because of malaria. Exa is the memory of a girl whose name was Ofelia. Padre Matías is the evocation of Padre Avila, who was priest in the parish of Santa Lucia. Ramón Balam is the caretaker at my house. Tia Charo is a caricature of my own tia Charo. Tia Micaela bears the stamp of my grandmother's cook.

Canek, for better or worse, is the book which best reflects my suffering for the suffering of the wretched, the Indians of my native land. If it should awaken any reader to a consciousness of injustice, I would be satisfied.

Ermilo Abreu Gómez

---

*The author's history of printings appeared in 1969. The most recent edition in Spanish [1977] is the 34th.—*Trans.*

CANEK

for María Asúnsolo

...of the general and bloody massacre which threatens the Province because of the uprising of the Indians of the region, who rushed into the reckless act of proclaiming one of their own number king, giving him the name of Canek.

—Municipal Council of Mérida,
17th of December, 1761.

Bitterness will overflow and abundance will dry up. The land will burn and the war of oppression will rage. It will be the time of suffering, of tears and of misery.

—Prophecy of Napuc Tun

There is no truth in the words of strangers.

—Prophecy of Chilam Balam

THE CHARACTERS

... when they came looking to see if the earth was good, the villages which had not had them were given names, and so were the wells, so that it could be known where they had passed....

from The Book of the Lineages
of the Mayas

1

Jacinto Canek got up before dawn. It had rained so much during the night that the yard in front of his hut had flooded. At the edge of the well he met an Indian.

Canek spoke to him. "It has rained hard, my son, and it will rain again because this is the rain of Giaia. Giaia was a man not from here, but from the east. But everything from the east belongs in spirit to the Yucatán. It will rain again."

No sooner had Jacinto Canek finished speaking than the rain started to fall. They took shelter under a palm and Canek continued. "You should know that Giaia had an evil son named Giaial. Giaial wanted to kill his father. The old gods whispered in Giaia's ear and told him words of vengeance. Then Giaia killed his son Giaial. He took his body and cut it up and put it in a gourd and hid it on a hillside. From time to time Giaia would take the gourd in his hands and cry tears of grief over it—because he had loved his dead son very much. And it came about one day that when he picked up the gourd he saw fish falling from it. He was afraid because he didn't understand what this sign meant and he fled from the spot. Then four brothers who were orphans came along and wanted to eat the fish. But as fate willed it, Giaia returned in time. The brothers ran off, letting the gourd fall to the ground. And from its pieces gushed torrents of water. There was so much water that all of the land for many leagues around was flooded. Then rain clouds appeared overhead. Everything was covered with the water from below and the water from above except the land in which we live now and a few distant lands which lie where the sun rises."

Jacinto Canek finished speaking and the rain continued falling.

Poor little Guy. He is the nephew of the hacienda owner and no
one loves him. He seems like a simpleton. His family has sent him to
the country to take the sun, to eat healthy food and to enjoy himself.
That is what his family said. Actually, they've sent him to the country to get him out of the way. He is so thin, he says such strange
things, he has such silly ideas that he bothers them. His brothers have
begun to say that he isn't really one of the family. When Guy hears
this, his eyes fill up with tears, but he doesn't say anything.

"He'll do fine at the hacienda," said his aunts. They were im-
posing women, tall and dry, the most fastidious members of the
household, always hovering about to make sure the sideboard was
dusted, the candelabras lustrously polished and the flowers well
watered. They brought Guy to the hacienda and left him. He has
been alone for a month. Canek has become his friend. He has given
him a conch shell and Guy amuses himself with it for hours and
hours. He puts it to his ear and remains absorbed, his eyes wide,
bright, misty. Guy's soul travels along the invisible trails of the wind
and the sea. Then, in the red earth, with his weak fingers, he writes
strange words which Canek does not dare erase.

One of Guy's aunts, Doña Charo, came to the hacienda. When
she arrived she was pettish and wheezing. She passed the day sitting
in the drawing room drinking tea and taking peppermint lozenges.
Suddenly, arms waving, breast thrust forward, skirts flying, she ran
out and took refuge in the living room. A hundred times over she
said she did not want to see any more Indians, least of all *that* one,
the horrible, skinny one who looked like a broken stone. When she
said "horrible," Doña Charo covered her face and blessed herself
and muttered, "Those hands all gnarled, the swollen eyes, the feet
full of sores, the cracked skin...."

Canek told her, "Child, that's only because the man works in
the lime kilns, in the tobacco dryers, in the marshes and in the salt
pits."

4

No one, not even Canek, knows who Exa is or where she came ~~from~~. She just appeared one morning, ambling among the pigs. Her ~~fa~~ce was grimy, and her hands dirty. At noon they saw her carrying ~~wa~~ter to the troughs in the corral. She even scattered handfuls of ~~o~~range blossoms there. She smiled. In the afternoon, since there was ~~n~~othing for her to do in the fields, she sat by the Indian women in the ~~ki~~tchen and set to work removing the kernels of corn from the cob. ~~S~~he filled her apron with the grains: white, black, purple, and blue ~~k~~ernels. She scooped them up and let them fall between her fingers. ~~S~~he smiled. At night she huddled in a corner of the pantry. The next ~~d~~ay she undertook the same tasks—wandering among the pigs, carry-~~in~~g water and degraining corn. There was only one difference: now ~~w~~hen Guy gave her a tortilla spread with lard she ate it.

5

Padre Matías would say mass in the afternoon. And he would ~~al~~ways include a sermon. In the sermons he didn't speak of doctrine ~~or~~ of miracles: he preferred to talk about the injustice of mankind. ~~Th~~e church would fill up with people; that is to say, with Indians. ~~Th~~e wealthy stayed home and grumbled. To those who criticized his ~~co~~nduct, Padre Matías replied, "For your information, the bishop ~~ha~~s given me permission to do this."

The offerings he collected for the church he distributed among ~~th~~e Indians. To those who demanded explanations for this, he said, ~~"F~~or your information, Padre Matías has given Padre Matías per-~~mi~~ssion to do charity in the best way he can think of."

6

In Tía Micaela's kitchen there was a gathering to celebrate the ~~arr~~ival of the rains from the east. Old friends came together by the ~~he~~arth: Ramón Balam, Domingo Canché, the grandson of the de-~~cea~~sed Juan José Hoil, Guy, and Jacinto Canek. Exa stirred up the fire under the nixtamal. They spoke very little.

Tia Micaela said, "These early rains are the sign of a long dr season. We must fill the tanks and throw in burning coals to kill th flies and gnats."

Then she got up and dissolved some cakes of pozole sweetene with honey in clay cups. It was raining and the water ran in torrent through the ditches in the patio.

CLOSENESS

*And it happened that blessings without
number sprang from a single blessed stone....*

from The Book of the Mayan Spirits

1

Tia Charo and the boy Guy eat together by the kitchen bell. The kitchen is full of clear vapors. They eat slowly and hardly talk. The cups of soup and of chocolate give out a sharp and sweet spicy smell, like clove and burnt almond.

Without looking up, Tia Charo sniped, "You really are a silly. Preferring vegetables to venison."

One of the fawns in the corral, a small domesticated deer with wet eyes, was watching them from the window. Canek and Exa were stroking the pretty, almost childlike brow of the little animal.

Tia Charo repeated, "You really are a silly, silly."

2

Tia Charo said to Canek, "Jacinto, go look for Guy. It's been a half hour since he went to the bin for a handful of corn."

"Here I am, Tia," Guy announced.

"It is a mere ten steps from here to that corn bin, boy."

"By day, yes. But by night, Tia, it's at least twenty."

Tia Charo crossed her arms. Canek raised the wick on the oil lamp.

3

The minute he came in the house, Guy said, "Tia Charo! I've just seen the *Xtabay*."

"Don't talk silliness, child. The Xtabay is a superstition of the Indians."

"I saw her on the road," Guy went on, "behind the ceiba tree next to the waterwheel. She's like a tall girl, pale and fair. She looks as if she's on fire inside. Her eyes are clear like water and her mouth is like an open pomegranate."

Tia Charo glanced toward the window and screamed. Canek was cleaning off a bloodstain which ran along the windowsill.

4

At the hacienda only Tia Charo and her invited guests get to drink the rain water cooled in clay jugs. The Indians drink the limy water from the wells, which is thick with the bodies of tiny vermin.

Canek was taking his afternoon nap under the portico of the main house. Guy approached him with a jug and said, "I'm not thirsty, Jacinto. Here, drink."

And in silence Jacinto drank that undiluted lightness.

5

Canek and Guy are in good spirits and off playing innocent games. Canek has made a little rabbit out of a white handkerchief. The little rabbit moves its ears, turns over and goes to sleep in his hands. Suddenly it starts, jumps down and runs away and disappears happily in the shade under the trees. Guy stares, his pretty green eyes open wide, and he smiles.

6

Jacinto Canek is in good spirits. In the late afternoon he has seated himself by the hacienda's great waterwheel. With him are his old friends Domingo Canché, Ramón Balam and young Guy. The murmur of the water running in the ditches carries the fragrance of shade. On the water surface the blossoms off an overhanging lime branch spin apart.

Canek says, "Who can tell me what holes the sugarcane sings through?"

His friends laugh.

"Who can tell me what is braided in branches?"

His friends look at him.

"Who can tell me the meaning of two green stones and a raised cross?"

His friends fold their arms.

Canek wrinkles his forehead and smiling says, "It's clear: the holes are the holes in a flute, it's the iguana that entwines itself in a tree, and the stones and the cross are the eyes and nose of a man."

7

On the hacienda there occurred a near tragedy which contained elements of both the mundane and the celestial. The rage that filled Tia Charo nearly killed her. Her face turned bright red and her clenched fists went white. She was overcome with swooning. Here is what happened: Guy, loyal interpreter of his aunt's faith, brought on the disaster. At just the wrong moment it occurred to him to take the statue of San Bonifacio to the storehouse so the saint could exercise his power against the plague of rats. But it happened at that moment the rats were either rebellious or going through a period of atheism. Anyway, they finished off San Bonifacio down to the last innocent crumb. They gnawed him from pate to toe. That was the source of Tia Charo's holy wrath.

After things had quieted down a bit, with a wink toward Guy, Canek attempted to explain what had happened.

"Calm yourself, little Charo, calm yourself," he said. "It must be the case that the statue wasn't blessed. And so not only couldn't the saint work against the rats, but the rats were aware of the impunity they enjoyed and took revenge for all the wrongs they have suffered."

8

Canek and Guy went out to hunt. Canek carried the bow and Guy the arrows. They were headed for the rabbit burrows. They went through the brush and on toward a rocky clearing. When Canek asked for the arrows Guy with his sweet rabbit's eyes timidly showed him the empty morral. Canek didn't say a word and the two of them set off for home whistling.

9

Stretched out on the ground, Guy watches the clouds pass by. He has been that way for hours, absorbed in their travels. Canek is there too, bathing Guy with his good smile.

"See the clouds, Jacinto?" Guy says. "There are spirits that live inside them. While the spirits are asleep, the clouds are white. They float slowly so as not to wake them. They cradle the spirits and carry them along. When the spirits awake, the clouds turn gray and crouch along the horizon. When the spirits get angry, then the clouds turn black, they crack and explode."

Canek asked, "And these spirits never leave the clouds?"

"When they leave, the clouds disappear."

"Then what *are* the clouds?"

"The clouds, Jacinto, are the shadows of the spirits."

Canek smiled his good smile, content as any saint in the church. Overhead the white clouds floated by. The spirits were sleeping.

10

The sun dissolves in a fiery wind.

"Not a cloud," said Canek. "If we don't get rain soon, the harvest will be lost."

The next day Guy made a fire and began to puff violently. With his hands he scattered the rising columns of smoke.

Canek asked him, "What're you making?"

"Clouds, Jacinto, clouds."

11

The two arrived limping: Guy and the sweetest of the puppies that had been born in the patio. Guy had a bandaged leg and the puppy a foot wrapped in cloth. The two moved along in jerks. The puppy whined, perhaps in pain, and wagged his tail, perhaps in gratitude.

"We fell down, Jacinto."

"I see, Guy."

"The puppy twisted his little foot. So I fixed it."

"And you?"

"Come here. Don't tell anyone. There's nothing wrong with me. I bandaged myself just to make the puppy feel better."

12

From the edge of the well arose the clamor of the crowd. The rope for bringing up water had broken, and the bucket was down at the bottom of the well. They couldn't afford to lose it. Time and again they threw in the hook. The prongs stirred up the lime and got tangled in the weeds, but the bucket wouldn't come up. It was a bucket carved of black wood. The master would notice it was gone. The workers lowered Canek into the depths. His voice sounded muffled, as though it came from the bowels of the earth.

When Canek came up he said only, "From down there you can see the stars."

13

Guy told Canek, "Listen, Jacinto, the bucket has fallen into the bottom of the well."

"Again?"

"I'll go down for you."

"Will you?"

"I want to see the stars too."

14

Guy asked Canek, "Jacinto, the dust that settles on the windows, the statues of the saints, the books and the canvas of the paintings, where does it come from?"

Canek answered, "It comes from the earth, little Guy, like everything in this life."

Guy said, "I don't believe it, Jacinto. The dust on the windows, on the saints, on the books and on the paintings doesn't come from the earth. It comes from the wind. It is the wind itself, that dies of tiredness and thirst in favorite, out-of-the-way places."

15

Guy couldn't make himself understood with Patricio, the grandson of Juan José Hoil. Guy spoke only Spanish and Patricio only Maya. Shy, keeping apart, they went out into the corn together. All of a sudden there was a snake right in front of them. Without a thought they took each other's hand.

Canek killed the snake.

16

Canek said to Guy, "Look up in the sky. Count the stars."

"They can't be counted."

Canek went on, "Look down at the earth and count the grains of sand."

"They can't be counted either."

Then Canek said, "Even though it isn't known, there *is* a number to the stars and a number to the grains of sand. What exists and can't be counted but we still feel here inside must have a word so we can talk about it. The word in this case is 'vast.' A word soaked in mystery. Having the word, you don't have to count stars or grains of sand. We've traded knowledge for feeling, which is also a way of getting inside the truth of things."

17

In the afternoon Jacinto and Guy left the village. They took the old road in the direction of Xinum, where the chiefs of the old Mayan rebels used to meet. From time to time the land grew dark. All at once there appeared the bird that guards roads which the Indians call *pujuy*. He strutted back and forth before them as if he were human and understood the weaknesses of men.

"Just the right time for the *pujuy* to join us, Guy. We have to go on, conquer exhaustion, fear, desire. Tiredness disguises its intentions. In travelers it appears as sleepiness, waywardness and distraction. Open your eyes wide, my boy, and follow the *pujuy*. He won't go wrong. His lot is like ours: to keep traveling so others won't lose their way."

18

Canek said, "Take off your hat and kiss the ground. Beneath us lies the body of Juan José Hoil. He lived a while here in Chumayel. He was skilled in the art of writing. His grandfathers handed on to him the experience and the events of the past. He wrote it all down in a book, which is hidden away in a steel-latched strongbox made of *jabin*. Some day you can read it and you'll come to know the secrets of his words. But you should be careful about what he says because out of fear of the whites he told it all in parables. That's the way we've had to guard our spirit so it wouldn't be destroyed by those who have let greed cloud their eyes."

19

In another place Canek knelt down and kissed the earth. Guy asked him, "Why are you doing that?"

Canek said, "Nachi-Cocom was buried here, hounded to death by the whites' cruelty. In the silence of the night the thunder of his voice can be heard from his grave."

Guy said, "I don't hear it."

Canek said, "That's because of your innocence."

20

One of the flowers in the garden, the one Guy's mother had taken the most care of, began to fade. One morning it was dead. Tia

Charo cut it and threw it out. Guy picked the flower up and placed it in a little wooden box. Without saying a word he buried it in a corner of the patio. Over the mound he placed a cross. He asked Canek to water it.

Tia Charo denounced what Guy had done as an act of heresy. She tore out the cross and stomped on the grave.

21

Tio Ramón, who lived on a distant ranch, came one day to visit the hacienda. He gave Guy a little dove as a gift. The bird was sweet and docile. She ate out of Guy's hand and, if he asked her to do something, she obeyed. Guy spoiled her so that he even allowed her to sleep in his room. But one day, no one knew why, the little dove took ill. She became sad, stopped eating, folded her wings, bowed her head and died. Guy mourned her.

When Tio Ramón learned about it, he brought Guy another little dove. Guy looked at her and he kissed her and then he gave her back to his uncle.

"Tio Ramón," he said, "I want to ask you a favor."

"What's that?"

"You aren't going to want to do it."

"Go on."

"Look: take the dove and tomorrow bring her back and tell me it's the same one that you brought me when you first arrived. What's more, tell me it isn't true that she died."

Tia Charo said to Tio Ramón, "If you do what this little dunce wants, I'll know you're a bigger dunce than he is."

Canek said, "Do it, Don Ramón."

22

Tia Charo sniffed at the meat that they had brought from the marketplace and wrinkled her face in disgust. Then she said, "What a pity. But, we can give it to the maid to eat."

Guy overheard her plan and said nothing. He hung around the

kitchen until he could ask the maid for a piece of the meat. Tia Charo surprised him while he was eating it.

"What a greedy child, taking food from the mouths of the servants. Hypocrite!"

Canek also ate a piece of the meat.

23

Every morning Tia Charo would become upset because the servants wouldn't get up when the sun got up.

"Idlers," she said over and over.

Very early in the morning the sun came in through Tia Charo's window. As soon as it was light, she got out of bed and immediately got ready to begin her work. Her major responsibility was badgering the servants. Guy was always making excuses for them.

"Tia, remember that last night they didn't get to bed until after midnight."

"They're lazy."

Tia Charo became ill. The doctor advised rest. And Guy, ever solicitous, hung a dark cloth over the shutters at her window.

"So the sun won't come in so early and you can rest better, Tia."

Tia Charo gave him an affectionate pat and sighed, "You really aren't such a bad boy."

She no longer scolded the servants about getting up with the sun. Now when she came out of her room, they were already about. So now she always remarked, "Louts! You've woken me up with your racket."

Canek started to go around without his shoes.

24

Tia Charo said to Guy, "You are your father's child. Just like him, absolutely no feelings. The only difference is he was a drunk. And doubtless you'd already be one, too, if you were old enough to drink. Probably you'll end up like him, writing that nonsense he called his 'poetry.'"

The rest of the household was in bed when Canek, tiptoeing cautiously, came to look for little Guy. He hugged him and with his apron wiped his eyes.

Canek put Guy to bed and covered him with a cotton sheet.
"Do you want a little milk?" he asked.
"No. Good night," Guy answered.
In a little while Canek returned with a glass of milk fresh from the cow. Guy drank it and then cleaned off his lips with the back of his hand. Then he asked, "Weren't you afraid out there in the corral?"
"The moon has come out, child. Go on to sleep."

From the window of his room, Guy talks with the children of the hacienda who have come to see him. Guy tells them something which has them gaping. What he tells them is this:
"Then my father, when he saw that the alligators were coming out of the river and that the Indians couldn't get away because they were tied to some trees, leaped off his horse and raced over. He didn't have a weapon, not even a machete. The desperate Indians began to shout. They were going to die. You could hear the alligators scrambling on the rocks. In a flash my father climbed to the top of a coconut tree. He grabbed a coconut and threw it at the closest alligator. That stunned him. Then he threw another one at the next alligator. Then at the one coming up behind that one. Then another and another. The alligators were thrashing around in their own blood. They were blinded and they stumbled around and they fell. The Indians had been saved. Then my father climbed down from the coconut tree and untied the Indians."
At that moment, Tia Charo stuck her head out the window and demanded, "Where'd you get all those lies?"

Canek answered, "They aren't lies, señora. You can still see the tracks of the alligators that died there."

28

Guy has a visit from one of his brothers. Older than Guy, his name is Gonzalo and he dresses like a little gentleman. He is what you would call a good child. When, through carelessness, he happens to do something wrong, he's the first to accuse himself. And if Tia Charo bawls him out, he cries like he's supposed to—meek and contrite. He even cries without making much noise, covering his face with his hands and hiding his head in the corner. When it's felt he's cried enough, Tia Charo calls him over and pats his shoulder and tells him, "Now, now, that's enough. Go along and just see it doesn't happen again."

Or else, "Go on, take this and buy yourself something sweet."

Only Guy understands that these scenes take place every time his brother, little Master Gonzalo, wants candy.

29

Guy also has a visit from his sister Carmen. Carmen is a sweet child. Without complaining, she bears the bad temper of Tia Charo. Everything is taken care of with two words. Whatever happens, Carmen answers, "Yes, Tia."

She doesn't mean Guy harm, even though she finds it hard to overlook his strange ideas. Some of them make her smile and some upset her. Then she'll say, "Is that so?" or "If you say so."

One day she asked Guy, "Tell me, what was our mother like?"

Guy said, "You know I can't explain that to you."

But then, suddenly, he added, "Look, when you cry about something, try to look *through* your tears. Because I'm sure that's where Mother is, that's where you'll see her."

Afterward Carmen said, "Is that the reason you cry then?"

Today is the first day of the celebration of the Blessed Christ of the Blisters. The masons' guild makes its solemn entrance. All construction work has been suspended. No mason and no apprentice will work today. Atop buildings under construction they have placed crosses decorated with branches.

All the small fry gather in the churchyard. There they light fireworks, there they shout and run around. But mostly they just run around. Now more than ever because a *toro de fuego* has just come out from the sacristan's quarters. It runs crazy, throwing off sparks like a demon. Its eyes burn bright, its horns pop, its feet are afire and its tail bristles with sparks. And what a tail it has, long, long like the tail of a comet! Guy and Canek watch the fiesta from the flat roof of the main house.

Guy has seen himself in Tia Charo's mirror. He's looked and he's noticed that his beard is beginning to come out. A light beard, soft, almost invisible, more like a fuzz. Running his hand over it, without wanting to, he blushed. Then he smiled.

That same day, in the afternoon, when he came to the table, Guy was sporting a mustache painted on with soot. Everyone laughed at his notion. Sententiously Tia Charo said, "Look at the little upstart. Not even down on his lips yet and he's already painting on whiskers."

Proudly, haughtily, Guy twirled his imaginary mustaches.

Only Canek knew the truth.

An eclipse of the moon was under way. Tia Charo's servants were shouting, "The moon is being eaten! The moon is being eaten!"

Sitting in amazement on the ledge by the waterwheel, they watched the moon disappear. With sticks they began to beat on the wooden washtubs and the metal caldrons. They had to make all the noise they could so the moon wouldn't get devoured. Nobody could silence their raucous frenzy. Moment by moment the sky grew darker. As time passed a kind of fury overtook the people. They were as if possessed by a rare and ancient terror. Guy and Canek were among them shouting too: "The moon is being eaten! The moon is being eaten!"

In her room Tia Charo grumbled and cursed.

But when the moon was completely in shadow and the noise and the shouts and the crowing of the roosters and the barking of the dogs choked up everyone's throat with fear, then it was Tia Charo who began to beat furiously against the wooden bars at her window and began in a strangled voice to yell, "The moon is being eaten! The moon is being eaten!"

33

It grew dark in the cornfield. Guy stopped and said, "Did you hear?"

"It's the *pis*," said Canek, "the bird whose call is the same as his name. They say he invented silence. They say he created it with his voice. They also say that when silence becomes too great he can break it with his voice. And afterwards, restless, he makes silence over again. He remakes it with his cry. And so on forever."

34

Days have passed and still neither Canek nor Tia Micaela know who the girl Exa is or where she came from, but they love her now the way you love one of those little doves that appear and, so placid, like handfuls of breeze, sleep under the shade of the trees.

35

Guy said to Exa, "If you don't finish eating that tortilla, I won't take you to where my rabbits are."

"How many are there?"

Guy held up five fingers. Exa began to eat, but secretly she hid five pieces of tortilla in her skirt.

36

Under a night sky full of bright stars, Guy and Exa lay together in silence at the edge of a cornfield.

Aware without seeing, Canek smiled.

37

Guy wanted to hold within his hands the rainbow of colors formed by a crystal. But in the shade the colors would disappear.

"Jacinto," he said to Canek, "I promised Exa a present. But I think this is an impossible gift."

"Nothing is impossible, Guy, when the heart is pure."

Guy went back into the sunlight to look at the rainbow colors. He was so stirred that his tears fell on them. The colors of the rainbow were captured in Guy's hands and Exa had her gift.

38

Guy wiped away a tear.

Canek asked, "Exa?"

Canek put his hand on Guy's chest.

Guy said, "Exa."

And Exa left as she had come, on the hands of the wind.

39

Coming back to the patio, Guy asked Canek, "It isn't cold, is it Jacinto?"

"Last night I was cold, Guy."

"Well I woke up twice and I was sweating."

The next day, returning to the corral, he again asked, "Were you cold last night, Jacinto?"

"Colder than the night before, Guy."

"Well last night I slept without covers and I sweated an ocean."

The next day the newborn fawn slept under Guy's covers.

40

At sundown, Guy came out to the patio and sat at the edge of the well. He spoke and then waited for his voice to fall to the bottom. Then he listened with pleasure to the echo which came back to him diluted by the darkness, caressed by the distance.

Canek said that Guy's health was improving. Guy's aunts were of a different opinion.

41

When Guy came back from the field he was bent over like a broken cornstalk and was drowsy. Canek laid him down on the grass. He sat beside him and kept watch over his sleep. In the shelter of his care, Canek could feel the boy was resting. Without speaking it, in the peace of his closed eyes, Canek read the message of innocence that lived in Guy's spirit.

42

Guy can't sleep. The night is sour and the winds from the south beat heavily on the limy earth. A yellow dust clouds the stars. Guy can't stop coughing. Resting his head in Canek's hands he sometimes smiles. Canek tells him ancient tales.

43

As soon as he woke up, Guy asked for water. He had spent the night sweating and in pain. Canek took the jug with water collected from the morning dew and gave it to him.

Guy drank with an almost painful anxiousness. Afterward he asked, "Jacinto, why is dew water so good?"

"Because it is filled with light from the stars. And starlight is sweet."

44

"Is it true, Jacinto, that children who die are turned into birds?"

"I don't know, Guy."

"Is it true, Jacinto, that children who die become flowers?"

"I don't know, Guy."

"Is it true, Jacinto, that children who die go to heaven?"

"I don't know, Guy."

"Then Jacinto tell me what *does* happen to children who die?"

"Children who die, little Guy, awaken."

45

In the morning Guy was gone. Nobody saw him die. Between the strands of his hammock he looked asleep. On his pale, delicate lips a light smile also slept. In the corner, not making any noise, Canek cried like a child.

Tia Charo came near, touched his shoulder and said, "Jacinto, you're not family. Why are you crying?"

46

Canek recalled what Guy had written in the sand: *Mama, I want to be the guest welcome in your eyes.*

47

The death of Guy and the disappearance of Exa have saddened Canek's heart. A black flame shines in his eyes. He passes the hours sitting on the railing of the waterwheel. Next to him he has a shepherd's crook which he doesn't need. At times he gets up and walks beside the water channel. It's as if he were getting ready for a journey. Sometimes he talks. As if he were getting ready to make a speech. Sometimes he raises his arms. As if he were about to give orders.

THE DOCTRINE

He who understands will become ruler over the people.

from The Book of Proofs of the Maya

1

Canek said:

"Today the whites celebrate the feast of the founding of the city they built among the hills of the ancient T-Hó. We also should recall the histories of our lost cities. Thus in our secret hearts we should remember that the mystery of the city of Chichén Itzá, abandoned for so many epochs of the sun, was brought to light at just the right moment."

2

Canek said:

"The whites know nothing of the land or the sea or the wind here. Do they know whether November is a good time for bending down the cornstalks? Do they know that the fish lay their eggs in October and the turtles in March? Do they know in February to free children and other innocents from the dangers of the south winds? Nonetheless the whites enjoy the fruits of everything produced by the land, the sea and the wind here. Now we have to learn how and when we can free ourselves from this evil."

3

Canek said:

"The whites have made this land alien to the Indian. They have made it so the Indian pays with his blood for the air that he breathes. This is why the Indian travels endless roads sure that the way, the only way possible, the one which will enable him to find his lost path, is the way which goes toward death."

4

Canek said:

"It's good to know how different are the needs of the Indian and the needs of the white. For the Indian a *cuartillo* of corn is enough to keep him; for the white an *almud* is not enough. This is because the Indian eats and blesses his calm, while the white eats and, still restless, hoards all he can for tomorrow. The white doesn't know that a jar can't hold more water than the water that marks its rim. The rest spills over and is wasted."

5

Canek said:

"If you pay attention you can recognize the nature and the intention of travelers. The white appears to march. The Indian appears to be asleep. The white huffs and puffs. The Indian breathes. The white goes forward. The Indian goes away. The white wants power, the Indian rest."

6

Canek said:

"We are the earth, they are the wind. In us the seeds ripen, in them the branches wither. We feed the roots, they feed the leaves. Beneath our growing things run the waters of the *cenotes,* still fragrant from the hands of the virgin sacrifices. Over them hurl the voices of the conquering warriors. We are the earth. They are the wind."

7

Canek said:

"The future of this land depends on the union of that which is sleeping in our hands and that which is awake in theirs. Look at this child: he has Indian blood and a Spanish face. Look at him carefully:

notice that he speaks Maya and writes Spanish. In him live the voices that are spoken and the words that are written. He is neither of the earth nor of the wind. In him, reason and feeling are braided together. He is not from below or from above. He is where he should be. He is like the echo which, in the heights of the spirit, unites with a new name the voices which are spoken and the voices which are silenced."

8

Canek said:

"The masters are red. They call themselves white. But they're red. Red like the dawning stain from the east that brought them, like the fire which burst from their hands, like the gold which burns and leaps in their beards, like the words which explode from their mouths, like the sores of their gods, and like the scream of the young girls they rape with no regard for their innocence. The masters are red."

9

Canek said:

"It all depends on the place a man occupies on the earth. The fortune and misfortune of men can be explained if we remember what connection they have to the land. So we see that the Indians live *next* to the land. They sleep at peace on its breast, they know its voices and they feel the heat of its bowels. They sense the smell of the earth, the smell which enriches their journey. The whites have forgotten what the earth is. They cross it, crushing and battering its bounty of flowers. They are the wind that breaks and leaps over the face of the rocks."

10

Canek said:

"It all depends on the spirit. Some men have quick, impatient spirit. For them the morning is already the beginning of an after-noon. Some men have slow spirit, almost asleep. For them an after-noon is merely the continuation of a morning. There are also men whose spirit is very fast and for them all of the hours of the day are full. For them was created rest at night."

11

Canek said:

"The same meal can mean different things to different men. A handful of corn, for example, is for the white man a luxury, for the Indian a necessity. The white makes it a sweet morsel, the Indian his daily bread."

12

Canek said:

"Think how, through the passing of time, in these lands of the Yucatán there still exist cities which are unseen. In the ones that can be seen live the whites. They are cities of war and of scandal. Flee from their lure. If you fall into them you will deny all that is yours—your name—and you will live in the broad lap of evil. In the cities which are not seen but are there, no one knows where, live those who have been and the men who have proven worthy of the privilege of keeping their doors open."

13

Canek said:

"Do not ask for those who go out and do not come back. It is true that some do return, but they do not know they have. If you look in their eyes you will see something like a dark vision flowing deep within them. They live like sleepwalkers. They should have our sympathy because they possess the spirit of that which was and they understand the blindness of the life we live here."

Canek said:

"Why do they teach us to love a god who allows the whites to beat and kill us? Why do we have to kneel and chant contrition we don't feel? From now on we won't say it, because even saying it only with our lips, we do damage to our spirit."

15

Canek said:

"What is the difference which distinguishes man from beast? Some say it is the soul. But that is the opinion of the proud. Some say it is reason. But that is the belief of the philosophers. I say I believe more in another distinction. What most separates man from beast is the ability the former has to stifle and kill his appetite."

Canek said:

"Things neither come nor go. Things don't move. Things sleep. It is we who go to them. That is why memory is not just a tool of the spirit for calling up the past. Rather it is a skill which allows us in a moment to see what is in its essence outside of time. Memory allows us to rise to a state, not available to the mind alone, where everything is present. What I am telling you was explained to me with reasons and in the right words by my godfather—a man of much wisdom and few books. It is something I never understood, but which it pleases me to keep here in my heart."

17

Canek said:

"The truth is: *the word was born unto itself in the darkness.* Here we have to make clear the meaning of this statement. The word is not the sound which is spoken or heard. The word is a cradle for the creator spirit. In the turbulent darkness of time, the creator spirit, which always was, looked into his mind and from that moment was born the word. That is why every word should be felt in the depth of the breast so it will become an image of that other word born from the creator, mirror of the spirit.''

18

Canek said:

"When the word came, it was not alone. It was accompanied by its echo, which spilled out through the reaches of the earth. And the word and its echo made all things, from the smallest things here below to the infinite things above. In time, worm, man and star came together. These three beings had light which was an emanation from the deepness placed within them. This few know and almost no one feels. We are lucky if we're even aware this mystery exists.''

19

Canek said:

"The gods are born when men die. While men still had confidence there was no need for gods. Then men could confide to other men what was in their hearts and minds. They could give word to each other without fear. But when men hid themselves from each other in order to eat the fruit the fields gave for everyone, when men spied on other men for the pleasure of women, when they began to say in secret the things which should be said aloud, then the gods were born. That's why the gods are so much more powerful, more cruel and more distant, the greater the suspicion which separates men from other men.''

20

Canek said:

"We mustn't forget what can be read in the chronicle written by the ancient elder who was called Nabuk Pech. In it he tells how in the north the whites searched for men to serve them as slaves. In those places the Indians were without water, without land or animals. They were dying of hunger. And so, full of despair, they gave themselves up to the first who laid hands on them. Very different was the fury with which the Indians of the south defended themselves. Because here they had food to stay alive and to nourish the power of the spirit. Never say then that those Indians in the north were cowards. Understand that they were dead men who cried out from the edge of the pit into which they were about to fall. To see it this way does them justice.''

21

Canek said:

"In a book I read an argument about what was the greatest thing in the world. Some philosophers said it was the water, others the mountains, others that it was the sun and somebody, I don't know who, said it was the disdain men could show for riches. Doesn't it seem more right,'' Canek went on, "that the greatest thing in the world is not to disdain riches but to know how to make good use of them, so that the benefits don't rot in the hands of the wealthy or go to waste in the hands of incompetents?''

22

Canek said:

"In the books it is told what a prophet is and also what a poet is. We have been told but many have forgotten. It is good to recall. A prophet is the man who can look on the face of God. In that splendor he learns to distinguish truth from lies. Because of this it is given to him to speak about what will happen in the future. A poet is the man who receives in his face the look of God. Because of this it is given to him to distinguish beauty from ugliness. The prophets had leave to lead the men who will come. The poets have the right to lead the men who are. When they have understanding of suffering, both prophets and poets can do good.''

23

Canek said:

"In a book I read that in the old days, the rulers wanted to call together armies to defend the lands they governed. First they called up the cruelest men because they supposed that these were accustomed to blood. So they drew their armies from the prisons and the slaughterhouses. But it came about that when these people stood face to face with the enemy, they turned pale and threw down their arms. Then the rulers thought of the strongest—the water bearers and the miners. To these they gave armor and heavy weapons and sent them out to do battle. But again, the mere presence of the enemy put weakness in their arms and dismay in their hearts. The rulers wisely then turned to men who, without being either strong or fierce or bloodthirsty, were simply brave and had something rightly to defend —the land they worked, the women they slept with and the children whose laughter gave them delight. And when the time came, these men fought with so much fury they drove off their enemies and forever were free of their threats and harassment. And so I believe and I tell you that the same is happening among us. How can the white masters expect us to fight with terrible passion if it's only for their benefit and their haciendas and never in the cause of our own spirit?"

Canek said:

"Years ago I read books which told the history of this land. I read them with pleasure, I was caught up in knowing past events and in the way of thinking of people who lived then. One time my godfather told me, 'The books you read were written by the men who conquered this place. Look with care at the reasons they put on their pages, because if you accept them without question, you will not understand the truth of the land, but rather the truth of men. Still read them, so that you will learn to hate the lies hidden in the thoughts of philosophers and in the prayers of the devout.'"

"And so in those accounts," Canek concluded, "I learned to read, not the letter, but the spirit of the letter."

Canek said:

"Luis de Villalpando, Juan de Albalate, Ángel Maldonado,
Lorenzo de Bienvenida, Melchor de Benavente and Juan de Herrera
were the good friars of San Francisco who came to this land long ago
to preach goodness and to root out evil. They fought not against the
Indians, who received them with innocent souls and gave them welcome in their hearts and in their huts, but against the white men who
were hardhearted and deaf to spirit. Let us say the names of these
good men like we say a prayer."

In low voices, the Indians repeated the names: Villalpando,
Albalate, Maldonado, Bienvenida, Benavente, Herrera.

26

Canek said:

"For the human spirit, a clean vice is worth more than a stained
virtue. A clean vice can be a redeeming power. Hidden in it is an act
of courage. On the other hand, stained virtue always implies weak
desire. Certainly an act of cowardice."

27

Canek said:

"Some prefer the ideal, others reality. From this results strife
which festers in the spirit. Men never reconcile their points of view.
The most they can do is to dream the reality or live the ideal. And the
difference in desires goes on. But the men of this land ought to be
both more demanding and more human. They ought to want the best
reality—what is possible, what grows and ripens in their hands. That
would be living the ideal of reality."

28

Canek said:

"One time, in years gone by, they buried a child together with a deer. They were buried together because they had been friends in life. Near that place there passed, in silence and alone, a stretch of the river, one of the streams that now run frightened, underground. So a white tree grew up there, fresh and young, as though made of silver and rain. Under its branches mothers heard the voices of their dead children. By its roots the old people felt the sighing of their lost animals. This tree breathes sweetness. The Indians call it 'the good ceiba tree.' ''

29

Canek said:

"By the very act of being, all beings have attributes, expressions of their essence, voices which reveal their origin and their condition. The attributes of being are not a decoration nor a quality which comes by chance from outside. The attribute is like the vapor from boiling water: it is water and not water. Thus the attribute of the sea is pride, the attribute of the sun authority, the attribute of men dignity."

30

Canek said:

"Never take pride in the fruits of your intelligence. You are only master of the force you put into the growing. Of what results you are nothing more than a spectator. Intelligence is like an arrow: once it has left the bow, no one controls it. Its flight depends on your strength, but also on the wind and—why not say it?—on the fate which pursues it."

31

Canek said:

"They say the body is like a chest where the soul is stored. That's good. But at times the soul is so big that the body, like an anis seed, has to be stored in the soul."

Canek said:

"Never be afraid of your tears. Cowards don't cry. Only men. What's more, my son, tears always fall when you're on your knees."

33

Canek said:

"In faith the spirit rests, in reason it lives, in love it takes pleasure. Only in suffering does it acquire conscience."

34

Canek said:

"How old are you?"

The Indian answered, "When I was born the locusts hadn't come yet."

Canek then asked, "When did the locusts come?"

The Indian answered, "After I was born."

35

Canek said:

"Zamná slept on a rose. Kukulcán dissolved like a cloud on the horizon. The name of Zamná is said by the moon. Kukulcán's is said by the sun."

36

Canek said:

"Zamná represents the water, Kukulcán the wind. Zamná has a mother's womb, Kukulcán a father's daring. With her hands Zamná held together the loins of the earth. Kukulcán sowed in it the seeds."

Canek said:

"Give me your hand. Put it in this jar and tell me what you feel."

The Indian answered, "Cold."

"That's because you touched the back of the prophet."

Again Canek asked, "What do you feel?"

The Indian answered, "Hot."

"Because you touched the prophet's breast."

And when Canek left, the flame of his spirit remained burning in the men's eyes.

Canek said:

"And why do you want liberty if you don't know how to be free? Liberty is not a gift which is granted or a right to be won. Liberty is a state of spirit. Once it has been created, then it is free even though it lacks freedom. Irons and prisons can't stop a man from being free. To the contrary, they make him freer in the depths of his being. The freedom of a man is not like the freedom of a bird. The freedom of birds is satisfied by the to-and-fro rocking of a branch. Man's freedom is achieved in his conscience."

Canek said:

"And there will always be an enemy who hears me and, seeing me flailed, will think my words are the notions of a madman or a man who mouthes discredited ideas. To him I will say that whoever has learned much from the stars and forgotten much more about men doesn't know much about this land. And I will also tell him an old verse I heard my godfather say one day:

    'We do not call the *azor* cheap
    Because he builds a humble nest,
    Nor does who said it have to keep
    A crook's advice from being best.'"

INJUSTICE

*They were there on the feast of San Bernabé,
day of the battle of T-Hó, and it was
revealed that the Indians had to die because
they were heretics.*

from The Book of the Conquest
of the Maya

1

Day by day the sadness and the violence in Canek's heart grows. Once he spoke aloud his thoughts. Now he is nearly mute: fists clenched, he walks alone along the roads of thorns, of stone and sun. His shadow goes with him. In Canek's eyes the blood of the Indians burns. His shadow is red.

2

The caravan of servants left Izamal and took the cobblestone road down to the ancient city of T-Hó. The old women went in the carts and the young girls on foot. They were watched over by troopers and nuns. The troopers blasphemed and the nuns prayed. When, exhausted, they stopped dead in the road, the troopers and nuns drove them on.

Canek followed the caravan. From time to time he passed out corn soaked in honey to the Indian women.

3

On the butcher's platform, two peasants were cutting up beef. The blood of the beasts ran through the brick channels. Suddenly, affected by the nearness of the blood, the men turned against each other. They fought fanatically, covering each other with wounds.

Canek tried to bring them to their senses. The butcher pulled them away, saying, "Leave them alone. Let them finish each other off. This way there'll be more blood in the meat and more profit."

4

The foreman thrashed the hacienda's barber. He flayed his skin and dashed vinegar in the cuts. Later, like a docile animal, he came and sat in the chair to be shaved. The knife moved across the foreman's throat like a bolt of lightning.

Canek stood immobile, biting his knuckles.

5

The master's sons arrived at the hacienda. They were young men with pale white faces. They lisped. Mounted on black horses with ringing hooves and flashing manes, they came at a gallop through clouds of dust. The first thing they did was to loose their animals among the seedbeds and new plants. The second was to plunder the collection box in the church and gamble away the money. And the third was to abduct the daughter of Jesús Chi, foreman of the hacienda. They took her off, abused her, and abandoned her in the fields. Shamed, Jesús Chi hung himself from the window of the young masters' room.

Canek went out to get the girl. She was covered with dust and blood and spittle.

6

One of the young masters went along the road to the west. He felt fear breaking out across his temples. His mount galloped, striking sparks on the cobblestones of the road. On the horse's rump rode one of the dwarfs of the old Nohpat. The dwarf was heavy and cold like a tortoiseshell. His breath was like a gust of icy wind on the young man's neck. They went on and on into the night as if moving through a liquid space infused with silence.

The horse returned to the village riderless.

Only Canek would take the animal in hand.

7

The master sent for Patricio Uk. He asked him, "Is it true you're going to marry Rosaura, daughter of the dead Jesús Chi?"

Answering for Patricio, Canek said, "Yes sir, it's true. And I am going to witness for them."

"Even after what my sons did to her?"

Patricio said, "Yes sir."

The master grinned. "That's right. After all, why would you need a new one when you aren't even going to get a chance to use her?"

Two dragoons came looking for Patricio and led him away, hands bound, to make him a soldier. Canek stopped him and told him, "Marry her anyway, Patricio."

8

It was the season for sport, so the master invited the Mayor on a deer hunt. The Mayor showed up accompanied by the other officials of the town. They brought along with them a poet whom they called Barbado. This fellow was as picky as an aging damsel. He held the belief that Indians were simply buzzards plucked bald. The trappings of the hunt sparkled as they do in illuminated engravings: slingshots, arrows, guns and horns. A pack of hounds preceded them. They took the best Indian hunters along as spotters. All day the noise they made rang through the countryside. At the end of the afternoon they started home drunk. In front came Canek carrying the body of an Indian killed by a stray shot. Behind came other Indians loaded down with the game. The Mayor and the master and the town officials tromped through the blood of animals and a man. The poet kept repeating, "Well, at least it was only an Indian."

9

Canek asked the Mayor, "The reductions in tributes the Indians asked for, they weren't approved?"

"No. The Treasury has great needs and the Treasurer is making demands."

"But sir, the Indians live in misery. They're hungry. They've given everything. They have nothing left."

The Mayor smiled. After a pause he whispered in Canek's ear, "Just between us, tell me: don't they have daughters?"

10

Padre Matías is a friend of Jacinto Canek. The padre understands the wickedness of men and the innocence of animals. For him religion is not a job, it's his joy. In Cisteil where he lives, he dresses in a franciscan habit and wears leather sandals. He has a good nose for what's going on. He scolds the sinners and bestows blessings on the good. Sometimes, without revealing his source, he will slip in one of Canek's sayings. Once he gave the following advice:

"A shepherd doesn't distinguish between good sheep and bad. That's why he never consults with anyone about his sheep before going out against the 'wolf.' So it is we have to defend both good Indians and bad against the whites, who are the wolves of our land."

11

Don Chumín, overseer of the hacienda, found the courage to speak with the master. He spoke with his head down and his hat in his hands.

"Sir," he said, "this year's harvests have been good ones. The carts loaded with cotton have already left. The bins are full and the olive oil presses never cease to run. The sawmill is stacked high with oak and pine and walnut."

"So?" the master said.

"Sir, we are already in October and the Indians have only been given, on account, three yards of cotton and a pair of sandals each."

"No doubt you're a friend of this Canek," the master said.

The next day a new overseer arrived at the hacienda. A man of fewer words and less friendly with Canek.

12

The children of the dead Chi—Canek's *compadre*—have inherited nothing. The only thing they got from their father was a cow. The cow lives with them, by their side. The children's lives depend on the cow. She's the plaything in their mischief, the guardian of their shack, the honey for their mouths. The bailiffs came to collect the new tribute. Canek offered to pay them with his labor. The bailiffs laughed. They went inside, lassoed the cow and dragged her out of the corral. The cow resisted. She planted her hooves in the ground and bellowed. The bailiffs took with them the life of the children of the dead Chi.

13

The arrival of the Mayor in the town is greeted by skyrockets and bells. The Indians have hung colored flags along the road. They don't even know the Mayor's name. Since dawn the women have been bustling about the kitchen preparing fancy dishes, sweets and salads for the Mayor. They are convinced he must be some variety of churchman. The priest is all dressed up in his straw hat and carrying his cedar cane. As he walks his buckled boots squeak. He doesn't know anything. The master of the hacienda has ordered that the steps that go down into the *cenote* be cleaned. That's where the best part of the program will unfold. Five boys with their legs in the air beat the lime water on the steps. One of them slips and falls, cracking his head, and rolls into the well. To the children's horror, the master scowls—displeased because the blood has dirtied the precious steps of the stairway. In Canek's eyes there is blood: the blood of a child.

14

Domingo Pat had to flee the town. His protest against the authorities had brought on the wrath of the Mayor. The bailiffs had opened fire on him from the town hall. That night the caretaker wouldn't give him asylum. On the pretext that there were snakes, he had set the dogs. Pat fled to the fields, and soldiers came after him. Day and night they followed his tracks. By the end of the week they hunted him down in the back country like a wild animal. When the dragoons returned they were impatient to collect their reward. With hard, cursed looks of satisfaction on their gloomy faces, they presented Pat's sandals as evidence.

Seeing them, Canek smiled. "When an Indian dies like this," he said, "it's only that he stops walking on the earth. His spirit grows and flies from place to place covered in flames."

A messenger brought the news that in the neighboring village the Indians had set fire to the whites' quarter. Among the rebels was a man called Domingo Pat.

15

On his pastoral tour the Bishop graced the hacienda where Canek lived with a visit. The Bishop entered the hacienda surrounded by so much incense and so many prayers that he was nearly invisible. So they would look their best for the ceremonies, the Indians received new clothes. A foreman made sure they didn't get dirty. As soon as the Bishop was gone the Indians had to return the clothes. Another foreman folded each garment and stored it in a chest. The master of the hacienda was both devout and economical.

16

Three whites blaspheme before a red jaguar which lies suspended in a dream of stone. Canek warns them about their imprudence but the arrogant whites laugh at him.

In the morning, the red stone was even redder and a bloodstain was all that remained of the whites.

17

Miguel Kantun from Lerma is a friend of Canek's. He writes him a letter and sends him his son to make a man of him. Canek answers saying that he will make the boy an Indian.

18

In the morning they found an Indian from the hacienda hanging from the branches of an orange tree. The master had the fruit sold before anyone could learn what had happened. Canek cut the Indian down and dug a grave. As he was burying him, far from the cemetery, in the fields, it seemed as though he was sowing the seed of man.

19

It wasn't even dawn when the bells began tolling in the church at Cisteil. Padre Matías sat up surprised, put on his sandals, cinched his robe, and went out into the street to see what was going on. When he got to the church, he came upon a new priest taking charge of the place. The sacristan smiled. The fat new padre explained in a nasal voice that the Bishop could no longer tolerate the disturbances at the Cisteil church. The sacristan smiled. The tolling of the bells was broken by the crowing of roosters. Padre Matías fled to Sibac and Canek mourned his absence.

20

A hot dry wind blew across the land. It leaned against the stubble and chaff of the fields. The sky was on fire and, without sap, the branches broke under the sun. In the distance, always invisible, the turtledoves timidly sang their song. The mules that drove the great waterwheel lay fallen on the paving of the patio. Their stomachs were bloated as if they were dead. Lustrous flies swarmed at their sores. Along the walls the iguanas, their eyes popping, breathed in and out. High above slowly circling vultures watched over the bleak scene.

A man arrived with his unconscious son. Neither the well nor the tank had water enough to wet his temples. Canek pushed open the door of the church. The dampness sweetened his face and his breath. He took holy water in his hands and wet the little child's face.

The chicleros came to the village. There were six of them. All, even the living ones, were already dead. Canek took them in and, so as not to aggravate their wounds, wrapped their bodies in banana leaves.

The master noted in his ledger: "A hundred-weight of chicle."

22

The Indians imprisoned in the jails they took away to the quarries. There they were made to break rock. The hammers fell on the stone slabs. When exhaustion left their arms weak, the overseer's whip cut into the Indians' shoulders. Again the hammers fell on the slabs. Suddenly the oldest of the Indians fell over dead. The overseer kicked him in the ribs. Canek came forward and strangled the villain against the rocks. The hammers again fell on the stones. Red chips flew.

23

The blacksmith at the hacienda approached the new master and said to him, "Sir, the iron to brand the cattle is finished. Shall I make another one to brand the Indians?"

The master said, "Use the same one."

Canek broke the branding iron.

24

The notary noted in his ledger: "The hacienda was transferred for so much money, with its lands, wells, animals, Indians and equipment as is indicated in the margin. The new brand for the animals and for the Indians will be affixed by the buyer."

Canek fled with the Indians.

WAR

*. . . and they murdered the orphans, the
helpless and the widows who lived on without
the strength to live.*

from The Book of the Ancient
Maya Gods

1

At the meeting of the guild of masons devoted to San Antonio, Canek said, "All the money we spend on candles and incense—why not use some to cure the sick?"

A white merchant shouted, "Better we buy liquor."

The Indians got drunk. In the middle of the drinking, there was a brawl and the merchant who sold the liquor was killed.

Full of wrath, Canek smashed the image of San Antonio.

The whites yelled, "The Indians are in revolt!"

2

The hogs on the hacienda where Canek lived broke the fence of their pens and escaped. They fouled the wind and the road with the smell of their bellies and the dust of their feet.

The whites yelled, "The Indians are in revolt!"

3

The Indians of Sayil threw stones at the broadside announcing the increase in the tributes. The constable was wounded and an Indian was beaten. In reprisal, while the foremen were collecting the tribute, the magistrate ordered a gallows put up. He dictated that it be constructed on a platform in the churchyard. They tore down an altar in order to build it. The villagers timidly remarked on the threat. Nevertheless, in the morning there were two dead animals: in the noose a dove and, on the executioner's wheel, a chicken.

The whites yelled, "The Indians are in revolt!"

4

The white soldiers captured one of the servants from the hacienda. They took him to jail in manacles. The colonel treated him with flattery and loaded him down with presents. The Indian, childhearted, was amazed. He returned to the hacienda turned out like a dandy. He smelled of Rose of Castile. Canek grabbed him and made him see how he had been fooled.

"Don't tell the Indians what the whites have made you believe."

But the servant ignored Canek. The next day a body appeared outside the garrison. Next to it was a small bundle containing the clothes and the gifts the man had been given.

The whites yelled, "The Indians are in revolt!"

5

Night had already fallen when Ramón Balam and Domingo Canché reached the village by a shortcut. They were escaping the slaughter that the whites were carrying out among the Indians. Balam had received a machete wound in the back and was bleeding. Jacinto Canek said to him, "The prophesies of Nahua Pech, one of the five prophets of old, have come to pass. The whites will not be content with what they have. Nor with what they've won in the war. They will want even our meager food and our miserable huts. They will raise their hatred against us and will force us to take refuge in the hills and the backlands. Then, like ants, we will become scavengers and we will eat bad things, roots, jackdaws, crows, rats and locusts. And the rottenness of this food will fill our hearts with rancor and war will come."

The whites yelled, "The Indians are in revolt!"

6

The soldiers broke into the houses of Canek's Indian friends. If the Indian had a machete hanging on his wall, they killed him with a single blow. If he had no machete hanging on the wall, with a single blow they killed him.

The captain explained, "They're bound to have a machete someplace."

The whites yelled, "The Indians are in revolt!"

7

The wind came out of the hills of the Petén, flowed down through the jungle dragging along with it the foul air from the swamps and the chaff and dust from the threshing floors. It bent over cornstalks and ended up exhausted, sour and dense in the savannah of Cibac and the black sands of the beach at Motul. Among the tall, blind cypresses was heard the name of Canek.

The whites yelled, "The Indians are in revolt!"

8

The call to war which Canek sent to the villages of the Yucatán was not in writing. Balam, Canché, Pat, Uk, Pech and Chi took on their hands only the blood of Indians assassinated by whites.

9

In the face of the whites' treachery, Canek called together the Indian workers. Without a word he pointed at a table on which there were weapons and loaves of bread.

Some of them took the bread. To these he gave guns and told them to go defend their homes. Others chose the weapon. To these he gave bread and told them to defend the barricades. Others took both guns and bread. These, because he saw they were crafty, Canek made his captains.

10

While the dancing for Chacmol was going on, Canek gave out the weapons he had received from the east to the Indians gathered there. Some of the Indians said, "They're not many."

Canek answered, "The whites have the rest."

11

After preparing for the whites' attack, Canek thought about Guy. After a while he climbed some trees. The nests he found he removed to the safety of the eaves of the church. The birds fluttered tamely in his hands.

12

The countryside is at war. Along the horizon, the trails of the wind are burning. In the air the *tunkules* and *icoteas* and the shouts of Indians in arms are heard. White troops came to the village. It was silent, empty, and in the distance were heard the rumblings of war: the beat of the *tunkules,* the *icoteas,* and the shouts of the Indians in arms. The white troops fell upon the neighboring village. The place was silent, empty, and in the distance were heard the rumblings of war: the beat of the *tunkules,* the *icoteas* and the shouts of Indians in arms. The troops fell upon the conquered countryside. The countryside was silent, empty, and in the distance were heard the rumblings of war: the beat of the *tunkules,* the *icoteas* and the shouts of Indians in arms. In the shadow the name of Canek was voice and echo.

13

At dawn soldiers arrived in the village of Cisteil. The houses were deserted. In the streets the dogs that had lost their owners wandered about howling. The soldiers spread tar on the roofs of the houses. When the sun came up there were only smoking ruins. A burnt haze, bitter, green, thick, was in the air. Then they knocked down the doorposts and pulled out the blocks and sowed salt in the fields and closed up the wells and killed the doves that were returning to their cotes.

When the soldiers left in the evening, behind them like a white shadow, a denseness in the mist, walked Jacinto Canek.

14

In Tiholop they apprehended Indians who, forced to their knees, spoke the name of Canek. In Tixcacal they apprehended Indians who, on their feet, spoke the name of Canek. In Sotuta they apprehended Indians who, in their silence, spoke the name of Canek.

15

Because it gave asylum to Canek, the rancho of San José was burned by the whites. One of the captains wanted to let the Indians go, but the other captain said, "Leave them inside. A burned Indian makes good fertilizer."

16

In the barren outskirts of Sibac there are no stones for erecting a barricade. Signs of the whites can be made out along the red horizon. Canek, naked, his feet dug in, is prepared to resist. Padre Matías contemplates the chapel he has been building with his own hands. He tears it down and piles the stones in the road. He has given a stay to death.

17

Tia Micaela has not wanted to flee. She has stayed behind to bury the dead. She washes their faces with her tears. With her own hands she lays out the charred bodies. So that the dirt from the graves won't fall in their eyes, she covers them with leaves of *yantén*. She looks among the corpses for Canek's and, not finding it, she is pleased.

18

The white troops which had been pursuing Canek returned from the rancho of San Joaquín. One captain said, "I'm bringing in a herd of fifty animals."

Another captain said, "I only count twenty."

"The rest are Indians."

19

Canek knows it: in the plaza of Cisteil stones are bleeding next to the dead Indians. For the stones and for the Indians, the plaza was a field of battle. For the whites the plaza at Cisteil was a circus.

20

Canek thought it but he didn't say it. The Indians who were near him were aware of it. At the moment of attack the Indians in front had to wait until the enemy opened fire. Then the Indians who were behind would advance over the bodies of their dead.

21

The Governor of the province communicated to his superior that the rebellion of the Indians was cruel and that their chiefs moved by their animal instincts, had defiled faith, reason and Christian custom and that, because of this and as a warning dictated by prudence, they would undertake to punish the instigators with energy as well as with charity.

After he finished his report, the Governor asked one of his aides-de-camp, "And where is the rebel who is called Canek?"

The aide-de-camp went to investigate.

22

When they caught Francisco Ux, an elder of Tabi, he told them he was Canek and allowed himself to be bound to a woodpile. He was burned to death.

23

In the savannah of Cibac the soldiers captured Canek and his friends. One of the soldiers, Dogface by name, bound his hands.

"Captain," said Canek, "you don't have enough rope."

Dogface tightened the knot.

"It's useless, captain," said Canek, "you'll never have enough rope to tie the hands of all the people."

Canek smiled.

The blood flowed from his hands like a tender flame.

24

The soldiers came home singing hymns of devotion. Behind them, bound in chains, covered with dust and with blood, dragging their feet, marched the Indians taken prisoner at Cibac. Before them, Canek walked like a shield and a banner, his chest covered with blood and his hair blowing in the wind.

25

In the jail yard the captured Indians were whipped. The soldiers guarding Canek in his cell were left speechless: the stripes of his friends' lashes appeared on Canek's back.

26

The judges decided to cut off Domingo Canché's hands. The executioner was accustomed to killing Indians from behind. Face to face with Canché he became afraid. The machete fell from his hands. Canché picked it up and with one blow cut off his own hand. Then he returned the machete to the executioner.

27

So that Ramón Balam's soul would arrive more quickly in Hell, the executioner hung him with a rope soaked in oil. Since there was no oil in the garrison, he used oil from the church altar. In the quiet of the afternoon, Balam's body smelled of incense. A dove slept in the hollow of his arm.

28

Padre Matías was good to Canek. He visited him in prison, understood that he was innocent and made them take off his fetters. When Canek talked about the boy Guy, Padre Matías's tears fell on the Indian's knees.

29

When Canek climbed the gallows the men lowered their heads. Because of this no one saw the executioner's tears nor the condemned's smile. In Canek's blood the blood of the afternoon was white. For the people the stars were salt and the earth was ash.

30

At a bend in the road to Cisteil, Canek met the boy Guy. Together and without speaking they continued walking. Their steps made no noise and the birds did not flee before them. In the shadow their bodies were clear, like bright light burning in light. They kept on walking and when they reached the horizon they began to ascend.

GLOSSARY

The terms in *italic* are Yucatec Maya, rendered in Spanish orthography by Abreu Gómez. The rest are Spanish words not translated in the text of *Canek*.

almud: a dry measure used in quantifying corn, beans; about 0.8 liters

azor: a goshawk; *Falco palumbarius*

ceiba: the silk cotton tree, *Ceiba pentandra;* holy to the Maya, it produces bolls of fluffy white kapok which can be harvested

cenote: a natural well formed by the collapse of the limestone surface shelf, giving access to subterranean rivers; some cenotes in the Yucatán are mammoth in size and so deep the water can be reached only by constructing stone or log stairways down to it

Chacmol: red tiger; a small sculptured figure of a jaguar

chicle: sap of the sapodilla tree, used to make chewing gum; chicleros are men who work through the jungles collecting the sap

compadre: "co-godfather"; a reciprocal term of respect and reference used by parents and godparents to mark the formally sanctioned obligation relationship established at a child's baptism or other ceremonial occasions

cuartillo: a dry measure; a pint

Giaia: a native god of the Antilles (Cuba, Puerto Rico, Jamaica, etc.)

icotea: (sometimes *hicotea*) a small land tortoise; the shell can be used as a noisemaker, either beat upon as a drum, or made into a rattle

jabin: a native hard wood; *Pascidia piscipula;* also called "dogwood" or "May bush," though much larger than northern dogwood

Kukulkán: the Mayan name given to Quetzalcóatl, "the feathered serpent," a Toltec deity; the most prominent of the Toltec kings who reigned over the Yucatán from their seat at Chichén Itzá

morral: a carrying bag with a shoulder strap; a game bag

nixtamal: corn soaked overnight in lime water and then cooked in preparation for grinding

Nohpat: in Mayan mythology, a witch, sorceress, dam of numerous gremlins and dwarf spirits

pis: a native bird; possibly also the Mayan *Xkau*

pozole: a drink made of corn flour and water, sometimes with beans added

pujuy: the roadrunner bird

toro de fuego: a fireworks contraption made of wood in the shape of a bull, sometimes borne by a man inside and sometimes on wheels, which is set afire and "dances" through the crowd at the height of fiestas

tunkul: a hollow, drum-like wooden gong

Xtabay: a woman spirit in Mayan mythology; a siren, the *Xtabay* entices men and either steals their souls or lures them t their death, similar to the "Llorona" figure in other parts of Mexico

yantén: plantain grass

Zamná: Mayan creator deity; also possibly *Zamana,* parent of Itzamna, the "Mayan Zeus"; according to the *Popol Vuh* the creator fashioned mankind out of corn

25
26
38